ILLUMINATION

Library of Congress Cataloging-in-Publication Data
LCCN: 2016912702
Little, Sylvia Hawkins
Illumination: Lewis Howard Latimer
Thank A Black Man - 1

Summary: *Illumination: Lewis Henry Latimer* (bio poem). Latimer, born in 1884 to runaway slaves, had very little formal education, yet during his lifetime he obtained numerous patents; and was renown worldwide for his electrical lightning expertise. ISBN:978-0-9801061-9-0 (trade pbk); ISBN:978-1-941185-00-1 (hbk); 978-1-941185-01-8 (ebk). 1 African American inventors—Biography—Science and Technology— Juvenile literature. 2. Inventors—United States—History—19th Century—Juvenile literature. 3. Inventors—United States—History—20th Century—Juvenile literature. 4. Stories in rhyme.

Printed In the United States of America
First Printing 2016

Graphic Designer
Sylvia Hawkins Little

Editors
Grant F. Little, III
Greer Hudson Little
Eleanor Renee Rodriguez, Ph.D.

Publisher
Epic Press
P. O. Box 141624
Austin, Texas, 78714-1624
www.epic-press.com

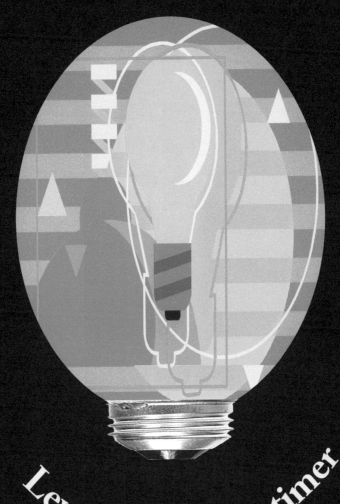

Lewis Howard Latimer

THANK A BLACK MAN - 1
Sylvia Hawkins Little, Ph.D.

A tribute to
my father and daughter,
Darnell H. Hawkins, Sr. and Lisa Little,
who used their time, talent and
energies to make a difference
for others.

Honoring "Black Difference's Makers"
Black men and women who through the years used their
ingenuity , time and energies to make life better for everyone.
We now give credit to many who often did not receive
it at the time and sometimes still haven't.

Stroll down any street,
    "Tell me? What do you see?
Examples of Blacks' ingenuity
    that make life better for you and me.

Many things are quite different
    from the way they use to be.
Things generally taken for granted.
    Things we don't often see.

Imagine how it was long ago
    on a dark and dreary night,
When candles, kerosene lanterns or gas
    lamps provided the only indoor light.

Lewis Howard Latimer
    made sure no one had to ponder.
An engineer, draftsman, legal expert,
    and inventor, he was a wonder.

The fourth child of George and Rebecca,
    Latimer was born on September 4, 1848.
His parents, runaway slaves, had traveled
    north and settled in Boston, a safe place.

During their travels North, skin color
    determined the roles they had to play.
Light skin George was plantation owner
    while dark skin Rebecca posed as his slave.

"I was one of the first pioneers of the electric lighting industry from its creation until it had become worldwide in its influence."

~Lewis Howard Latimer~

Shortly after Lewis' birth, his
  father's slave owner captured him.
He was determined to take him back to
  Virginia where his future was grim.

George's community, former slaves and
    abolitionists, rallied against his arrest.
Rasing funds to buy George's freedom,
    the solution they deemed the best.

The situation between his father
    and his owner gained great notoriety.
It went up to the Massachusetts Supreme
    Court before his father was set free.

Many believe the Dredd Scott Decision
    caused George Latimer to disappear.
Or his former owner caught him
    when he wasn't looking in his rear.

The Dredd Scott Decision in 1857
    placed on many slaves an unfair weight.
Without papers a slave couldn't be considered
    a freed man even if he lived in a free state.

From his boyhood background,
    it was unlikely to predict fame.
Yet, when he died in 1928, thousands
    knew Lewis Howard Latimer's name.

Before ten, he went to school and after
    school he worked in his father's barbershop.
After ten, he worked full-time with his
    father hanging paper and school stopped.

Leaving school early to work with parents was
    typical for children in the 19th century.
Unlike the South, education was free for
    all in Massachusetts but not compulsory.

Unable to support four children
    after her husband disappeared,
his brothers were sent to a farm school
    and his sister to friends to be reared.

Latimer stayed with his mother until
    she went to sea as a ship stewardess.
He went to join his brothers at the
    State Farm School because it was best.

Latimer hated manual labor working in
the fields; a farm school requirement.
When his brother William offered a way out,
he was happy to leave this confinement.

They traveled by night, slept during the day,
    and scrounged or stole food along the way.
Walking, running, or stealing railroad rides,
    covering 80 miles to Boston, side by side.

Except for the Underground Railroad,
    their journey to Boston, one might say,
resembled the trips runaway slaves made
    to freedom in the North, in many ways.

Arriving back in Boston at thirteen, job
    opportunities were few and far between.
Latimer took many odd jobs
    about which he wasn't too keen.

Joining the United States Navy at fifteen,
    Latimer fought in the Civil War.
Serving on the U.S.S. Massasoit gunboat,
    he honored the Union Star.

After the war, Latimer worked as an
    office boy for a patent law corporation.
Protecting inventors' rights was Crosby
    Halstead and Gould specialization.

An excellent reader and extremely
    skilled with drafting tools and pen,
Latimer emulated and surpassed
    the draftsmen sketches around him.

When his sketches of patent
    drawing caught his employers' attention,
Latimer was
    promoted to a junior draftsman position.

In one special aspect,
    Lewis Latimer was quite unique.
He worked with both Alexander Graham
    Bell and Thomas Edison—quite a feat.

When he assisted Alexander
    Graham Bell in 1876, time was tight.
To draft the patent's for Bell's
    blueprint, Latimer worked all night.

They got Bell's "telephone" patent
    application in with little time to spare.
A good thing because Bell's rival,
    Elisha Gray, wanted his patent there.

Latimer began in 1879 working for
    the U.S. Electric Lighting Company.
Thus began another stage of his destiny
    – illuminations allowing us to see.

As mechanical draftsman and secretary for
    Hiram Maxium, Edison's competition,
Latimer learned about electrical
    light construction and operation.

Before long the electric light
    bulb burn rate caught his attention.
Improvement became a necessity,
    then it was a reality, finally his invention.

Thomas Edison invented the
      electric light bulb, that is true.
However, Latimer's patent, 1882,
      made the bulb practical for you.

Edison's paper filament electric
      light bulb burned too fast.
Latimer's carbon filament electric
      light bulb was design to last.

*ANTIQUE REPRODUCTION OF CARBON FILAMENT

ELECTRIC LIGHT BULB AVAILABLE TODAY

at LightBulbs.com

Promoted to Chief Electrical
 Engineer, Latimer was in great demand.
His abilities in electric lightning
 became well known throughout the land.

Eventually, as more major cities
    began wiring their streets for electricity,
Latimer was requested to lead their planning team.
    He was the man to see.

Latimer traveled near and far sharing his
    knowledge on electricity.
For lighting government buildings,
    railroard stations and cities.

Philadelphia, New York City and Montreal's
    first electric light plants were more than whims.
Like Canada, London and New England's major
    thoroughfares' installation teams were lead by him.

In just one year, Latimer established
    Maxium's London Incandescent Light Factory.
He taught all aspects of light bulb
    making and the art of blowing glass for all to see.

In 1884, Latimer joined the Edison's
    Electric Light Company and realized his dream.
He became a charter member, the only African
    America on "Edison Pioneers", an elite research team.

Hired for his drafting, electrical engineering
      and patent expetise, Latimer was the expert witness.
For over 26 years, Edison's company won
      many patent litigation court cases because of him.

The first engineering handbook
      [1890] on lighting systems was penned by him.
Lighting engineers called, "*Incandescent Electric Lighting: A
      Practical Description of the Edison System*", his book a gem.

When Latimer
      died in 1928 one could say,
 his contributions made
      this world better in so many ways.

He was a wonder—*a son, brother, husband,*
      father, engineer, legal expert, inventor, draftsman,
author, poet, teacher, musician and philanthropist
      —a self-taught man, A RENAISSANCE MAN.

One of the most important
    Black inventors of all time.
Latimer is renown because his abilities
    with lighting helped the world shine.

The magnitude of importance
    for his most famous discovery.
Must not be overlooked,
    it holds an important place in history.

He was a wonder—*a son, brother, husband,*
    father, engineer, legal expert, inventor, draftsman,
author, poet, teacher, musician and philanthropist
    —a self-taught man, A RENAISSANCE MAN.

A few things to remember,
A few points to ponder!
Latimer contributions
show he was truly a wonder.

Without a doubt—as you trace
the progress of this great land
You'll have to take time to honor
and thank "a Black Man".

LATIMER'S PATENTS

U.S. PATENT NUMBER	DESCRIPTION	DATE
147,363	Water -Closets [toilets) for Railway Cars (with Charles W. Brown)	February 10, 1874
247,097	Electric Lamp (with Joseph V. Nicholas)	September 13, 1881
252,386	Process of Manufacturing Carbons	January 17, 1882
255,212	Globe Supporter for Electric Lamps (with John Tregoning)	March 21, 1882
334,078	Apparatus for Cooling and Disinfecting (Witnessed by Mary Latimer)	January 12, 1886
557,076	Locking Rack for Hats, Coats, and Umbrella	March 24, 1896
781,890	Book Supporter	February 2, 1905
968,787	Lamp fixture (with Charles W. Brown)	August 30, 1910

SOURCES:
http://edison.rutgers.edu/latimer/latpats.htm
http://www.ideafinder.com/history/inventors/latimer.htm

REFERENCES

Fouché, Rayvon, *Black Inventors in the Age of Segregation.* Baltimore & London: The John   Hopkins University Press (2003)

Hayden, Robert C., *9 African American Inventors.* Frederick, Maryland: Twenty-First Century Books, A Division of Henry Holt and Co., Inc. (1972)

Van Sertima, Ivan, *Blacks in Science: Ancient and Modern.* New Brunswick, New Jersey: Transition Books, 1984

http://african-americaninventors.org/

http://www.answers.com/topic/lewis-h-latimer

http://www.blackinventor.com/

http://www.eng.wayne.edu/news.php?id=2013

http://www.nps.gov/archive/edis/edisonia/graphics/10114016.jpg Founding members of Edison Pioneers at organizational meeting;1/24/18;{10.114/16}

http://teacher.scholastic.com/activities/bhistory/inventors/

GLOSSARY

Application—a written request; a way of being used; in computing, an application program.

Compulsory —must do, no choice, required. Education is compulsory up to certain age in all states.

Constitution— the basic beliefs and laws of a nation, state, or social group that establish the powers and duties of the government and guarantee certain rights to the people.

Construction—something built or put together; job or business of construction.

Contribution— to donate something, such as money, time or talent, to a common fund or group effort.Corporation—a group of people recognized by law and authorized to carry out certain functions with powers independent of the individual members.; any group of people who function as a unified whole.

Draftsman—a person who draws detailed plans and designs

Dred Scott Decision— The Supreme Court decision Dred Scott v. Sandford was issued on March 6, 1857. Delivered by Chief Justice Roger Taney, this opinion declared that slaves were not citizens of the United States and could not sue in Federal courts. In addition, this decision declared that the Missouri Compromise was unconstitutional and that Congress did not have the authority to prohibit slavery in the territories. The Dred Scott decision was overturned by the 13th and 14th Amendments to the Constitution.

Electrical—using or having to do with electricity; exciting; thrilling.

Electricity—electrical current; a physical phenomenon caused by the movement of certain charged particles such as electrons, especially between points having different electrical charges, and seen in naturally occurring phenomena such as lightning and magnetic attraction and repulsion.

Emancipation Proclamation—the declaration first introduced in 1862 by President Lincoln that freed all the slaves from Confederate states that were not yet under Union control during the United States Civil War.

Emulated—to try to be the same as; to follow the manner or pattern of; attempt to resemble; mimic. Excellent—extremely good; superior; of high quality.

Filament—in an electrical device such as a light bulb; a fine wire that lights or heats up when current is passed.

Illumination—the intensity of light per unit of area of a surface exposed to light, a light or lighting.

Incandescent—giving off light as a result of heating; very bright or glowing; showing brilliance or passion. Installation—to make ready for use; the act of installing or condition of being installed.

Magnitude—the measure of brightness; size, extent, or dimension; greatness or importance.

Mastered—to develop skill in or knowledge of something; expertness at.

Mechanical Drawing—descriptive precision drawing, often to scale, that is done with the aid of such implements as T squares, compasses, and French curves; drafting.

Observing—to watch closely or make a systematic observation of

Philanthropist—a person who give their time, talent, or treasure to make a difference in the lives of others.

Practicing—to do over and over; repeated performance in order to become skillful.

Renaissance man—a man who is knowledgeable, educated, or proficient in a wide range of fields.

Specialization—specific pursuit or field of study.

Surpass—to be better than or exceed in talent, accomplishment, or the like.

Thoroughfare—a street that opens at both ends into other streets.

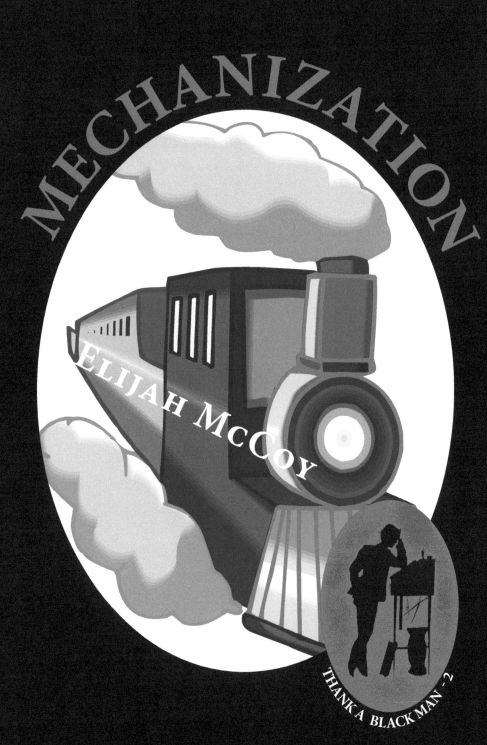

MECHANIZATION

ELIJAH McCOY

THANK A BLACK MAN - 2

Sylvia Hawkins Little, Ph.D.
http://epic-press.com

CPSIA information can be obtained
at www.ICGtesting.com
Printed in the USA
BVHW021257130920
588705BV00001B/47